Reinventing Insurance
The Emergence of Decentralized Blockchain Platforms

Table of Contents

Chapter 1. Introduction

In a world constantly reshaped by technological advancement, it's vital to keep a finger on the pulse of the new revolutions emerging from the digital ether. Our Special Report, "Reinventing Insurance: The Emergence of Decentralized Blockchain Platforms", is your perfect guide to decoding these advancements and understanding their implications. Navigating through the complex labyrinth of the blockchain technology might seem daunting, but this report breaks it down to its simplest for you. Not too techie, but just enough to give you a thorough understanding, it peels back the mystique surrounding this groundbreaking technology that is fundamentally transforming the insurance industry. Engaging and enlightening, this report promises an invaluable exploration of a futuristic landscape where decentralized blockchain platforms are reinventing how insurance operates. Are you ready to delve into the future of insurance? This is your ticket. Buckle up!

Chapter 2. Unveiling Blockchain: A Beginner's Guide

Our journey begins with an exploration of a technology that started its life as a ledger for Bitcoin, but has since found myriad applications across various sectors: the Blockchain. However, before we delve into the complex avenues of the decentralized ledger system, let's take a step back and comprehend the core participants of this technology, their roles, and how an unassuming ledger has been transformed into a foundational technology.

2.1. Understanding Blockchain

In its simplest form, the Blockchain is a time-stamped series of immutable transactional data that is managed by a cluster of computers not owned by any single entity or authority. The operative words here are 'immutable' and 'decentralized'. These sets of blocks (holding bundles of transactional records) are secured and bound to each other through principles of cryptography, forming a chain - hence the name, 'Blockchain'.

The system relies on a peer-to-peer (P2P) protocol and can be visualized as a kind of distributed ledger wherein transactional data is stored across the network of computers around the world, referred to as nodes. This means your data doesn't exist in one central database, but is instead distributed across hundreds or even thousands of nodes around the world, which is what makes Blockchain inherently secure, yet transparent.

2.2. The Building Blocks of Blockchain

So, what makes up a blockchain? Each block in a blockchain network stores some vital pieces of information that distinguish it from other blocks:

1. The data in the block, depending on the type of blockchain. If it is a Bitcoin blockchain, the block will record the details of the transaction like the sender, receiver, and amount of coins.

2. A hash, essentially the block's unique digital fingerprint. Even a small alteration in the transaction data changes this hash completely.

3. The hash of the previous block in the chain, thereby creating a chain of blocks and giving us the term "blockchain".

2.3. How Blockchain Works

Blockchain's genius comes from the combination of three technologies: cryptographic keys, a distributed network with a shared ledger and the incentive to service the network's transactions, security, and record-keeping.

A simplistic understanding of the process can be summed up in the following steps:

1. A transaction is requested.

2. The requested transaction is sent to a P2P network consisting of nodes.

3. These nodes validate the transaction and the user's status using algorithms.

4. Once the transaction is complete, it is combined with others to create a block of data for the ledger.

5. The new block, now attached, is added to the existing blockchain in such a way that it is secure and immutable.

So, once a block is added to the blockchain, it becomes publicly available for anyone to see, making it transparent.

2.4. The Immutability Factor and Consensus Protocols

One of the most talked-about properties of Blockchain is its immutability, or the inability to alter or delete any transactional data once it's added to the Blockchain. Although an essential feature, how does this work?

In comes the consensus protocols. A consensus protocol, as the name suggests, is the process of achieving agreement between all nodes on the true state of shared data. In the world of Blockchain, the commonly used models for achieving consensus are Proof of Work (PoW) or Proof of Stake (PoS).

With PoW, the solution to a complex puzzle is required to define the new block. In the PoS model, the creation of a new block is delegated to a specific node, proportional to its stake or wealth in the network.

Thus, once data is locked into a block via these consensus mechanisms, changing it would require an inordinate amount of computational power, thereby making the system secure and immutable.

2.5. Benefits of Blockchain

Blockchain technology offers groundbreaking benefits:

1. Decentralization: There's no central location where the data lives. Therefore, the system becomes highly resistant to cyber-attacks.

2. Transparency: All the transactions are public, yet the identity of the person behind a wallet address remains private.

3. Immutability: Once something is recorded on the blockchain, changing or erasing it is nearly impossible.

2.6. Blockchain in Insurance

In the subsequent sections, we will explore the implications of blockchain technology in the insurance space. Its decentralized, transparent, and immutable characteristics provide scope for efficiency improvements, cost reduction, and innovative business models in the insurance landscape.

As we navigate further in this report, fasten your seat belts as we delve into the disruptive potential this technology holds for an industry as old yet as essential as insurance. While it's just the beginning and there are numerous hurdles to cross before Blockchain can overhaul our insurance systems, the potential perks suggest the sweat and grind would be worthwhile.

With no single point of failure and its stringent cryptographic security measures, Blockchain is indeed setup to make waves in the near future and revolutionized traditional insurance models beyond recognition.

One parting thought - blockchain is not just an evolution; it's a revolution in digital technology. And, like all revolutions, it comes with its own challenges and opportunities. Through the following chapters, we will unearth them all. Together, let's decrypt the future!

Chapter 3. Blockchain Technology: Disruption in the Making

Technological advancements have been a harbinger of disruption in many sectors–the insurance industry is no exception. The emergence of blockchain technology has cultivated new models and methods, teetering on the brink of revolutionizing the way the insurance industry traditionally functions.

3.1. Prologue to Blockchain

Hailing from the realm of digital currencies, the blockchain is, in essence, a deceptively simple concept. A blockchain is a continuously growing list of records, known as blocks, that are linked and secured using cryptographic principles. Each block primarily contains a cryptographic hash of the preceding block, transaction data, and a timestamp. Its design inherently resists data modification—once the data has been recorded in a block, it becomes extremely arduous to alter.

Initially conceptualized for transactions of the cryptocurrency Bitcoin, the robustness of blockchain technology quickly extended its utilization beyond the confinements of digital currency proceedings. Its unique features such as decentralization, immutability, security, and transparency have opened doors to numerous applications across varied industry verticals, where the insurance sector is no outlier.

3.2. Blockchain: The Game Changer in Insurance

Insurance, as an industry, is wrought with multiple challenges. It deals with laborious processes, complex contracts, potential fraud, and lack of trust. Blockchain technology, with its inherent attributes, is ideally suited to address these issues.

3.2.1. Decentralization: A Potential Solution to Fraud and Trust Issues

Blockchain's decentralized nature means that information is stored across a network of computers globally, known as nodes. These nodes collectively validate new transactions and record them on the blockchain. This decentralization eliminates the need for a central authority or intermediary. Consequently, it grants the process enhanced transparency and traceability, endemic for establishing trust among parties involved in insurance contracts.

Furthermore, blockchain's cryptographic audit trail makes it nearly impossible for anyone to modify past claims or transaction records, thereby significantly mitigating insurance fraud, a pervasive problem the industry has been wrestling with.

3.2.2. Smart Contracts: Streamlining and Automating Claims Processing

Another groundbreaking application of blockchain in insurance is the implementation of "smart contracts". A smart contract is a self-executing contract embedded with the terms of the agreement between buyer and insurer being directly written into lines of code.

An insurance policy built as a smart contract on the blockchain automatically validates a claim and triggers a quick, automatic payout without the need for a manual claims assessment. This not only slashes administrative costs and claim handling times but also heightens customers' claims experience.

3.3. Case Studies: Blockchain in Action in the Insurance Industry

Numerous insurance companies have holistically embraced this technological revolution to enhance operational efficiency, customer experiences, and risk management. Here are some illustrative entries:

3.3.1. AXA's Fizzy: Automated Flight Delay Insurance

AXA, a French multinational insurance firm, pioneered a blockchain-based insurance product called Fizzy. If a policyholder's flight is delayed by more than two hours, this Ethereum-based smart contract automatically triggers reimbursement. Notably, the underlying source of data for flight delays is tamper-proof, augmenting the credibility of the process.

3.3.2. Guardtime: Transforming Health Insurance

Guardtime, a software security company, partnered with Estonia's eHealth Authority to secure health records on the blockchain. With their Keyless Signature Infrastructure technology, they ensure the immutability and real-time auditability of health records, thereby providing proof of integrity, mitigating fraud, and improving data handling processes.

3.4. Challenges and The Road Ahead

Blockchain carries immense potential in reshaping the insurance landscape. However, it's not without challenges. Regulatory hurdles, legal uncertainties, technological complexity, privacy issues, and the need for a revamp of existing IT systems are some of the significant roadblocks.

Despite these challenges, the application and potential of blockchain technology in insurance are compelling. Insurers, who thrive on trust and the promise of stability, will find a powerful ally in the blockchain. It not only promises increased security, trust, and efficiency, but also heralds the opportunity to innovate in product development and service delivery.

The progressive integration of blockchain technology into insurance operations is not a matter of 'if' but 'when'. As we journey down this path of digital transformation, blockchain emerges as a robust companion, harbinger of a new era in the world of insurance.

Chapter 4. Understanding Decentralization and Its Import

The transformative charge powering the exhaustive world of blockchain technology starts with its decentralizing feature - a fundamental change from the traditional systems we've grown accustomed to. Decentralization, a term used ubiquitously in relation to blockchain, might sound complex initially, but it is relatively straightforward in its concept.

To begin, it's essential to understand the traditional system of centralization. Centralization refers to the concentration of control, authority, or activity in a single central point or organization. It's a model wherein decision-making is concentrated at the top, so much so, that even the slightest snag at this point can disrupt the entire system. Examples of centralization are easily found in everyday life - from our public health and education systems to major corporations and banks.

Unlike centralization, where power is metaphorically situated at the pinnacle, decentralization diffuses this power across the system. In a decentralized system, every node (participant or computer in the system) has equal access to all the information across the network, and decisions are made collectively.

4.1. The Relevance of Decentralization

The relevance of decentralization spans many folds. Foremost, it addresses the inherent vulnerabilities of a centralized system. As stated previously, if a centralized system encounters an issue, it can temporarily or indefinitely halt operations. This fault line in centralization is commonly referred to as a 'single point of failure'.

Moreover, centralization concentrates power thereby making the system prone to corruption and manipulation. The disconcerting 'too big to fail' conundrum articulated post the 2008 financial collapse is a stark reminder of centralization's perils.

Decentralization remedies these issues by distributing power, making systems more robust, and stimulating participation and cooperation among all stakeholders. In the housing of data alone, decentralization provides redundancy by storing copies of information across multiple nodes, enhancing security & reducing data loss probability.

The relevance also shines in the context of trust. In a centralized system, trust is imperative. For example, we must trust the banking institute when depositing money, or an insurance company when buying an insurance policy. This is not necessary in a decentralized blockchain system as the technology, fundamentally, is 'trustless'. This means transactions are transparent and verifiable by any participant without requiring trust in any third party.

4.2. Decentralization and Blockchain

The birth child of decentralized systems, Blockchain, is more than a mere technology. It is a philosophy, a rethinking of how society can organize, collaborate, and prosper without a centralized authority. Blockchain technology facilitates transparency, security, and efficiency, all while maintaining participant anonymity.

At its core, blockchain is a distributed ledger system where the ledger - a record of transactions or any valuable information, is maintained by several participants, or 'nodes'. No single node controls the ledger.

Instead, it works on a consensus mechanism where nodes agree on the validity of transactions.

This decentralized framework inherently fosters trust among the nodes. If a counterfeit transaction is presented to the system, nodes can verify and reject it based on transaction history spread across the blockchain. What essentially forms is a system built on transparency, accuracy, and self-regulation that is accessible and viable mirroring the virtues of decentralization.

4.3. Decentralization and Insurance Industry

The insurance industry, mired by the opaque hassles inherently tied to centralized systems, is ripe for disruption by decentralized platforms. By leveraging blockchain technology, insurance can undergo a revolutionary shift that addresses issues of trust, claims processing, and policy issuance through a transparent, efficient, and quick process.

For instance, in today's centralized insurance industry, trust is an issue. Often, policyholders don't trust insurers with their claims and dread the lengthy process of claim settlements. Decentralized platforms, using blockchain, cut out the need for intermediaries, automate claim processing through smart contracts, and make the entire process more transparent and faster.

In the final notion, it's not without merit to say that decentralization stands as the foundation of blockchain's disruptive abilities. Like the first step to a thousand-mile journey, understanding the concept of decentralization brings us to the threshold of blockchain technology's vast applications, like the reinvention of the insurance industry. This profound philosophy not only reshapes data handling and security but lays the groundwork for a society where trust is established not by centralized watchdogs but by systemic transparency and mutual consensus.

As we delve further into blockchain and decentralized platforms, our understanding of these subjects must mature. Continuous learning, researching, and understanding of this technology is the key to unlocking and leveraging its potential. This change is here, and it's disrupting our traditional systems. Are we ready to adapt is a question that remains to be answered. We hope you are up for this exploration into the future!

Chapter 5. Insurance Industry: Tracing the Evolution

It's almost impossible to discuss the rise of decentralized blockchain platforms in insurance without tracing back to the roots and unfolding the evolutionary timeline of the insurance industry. The path trodden by this industry reveals a perpetual progression, an unwavering determination to adapt, innovate, and modify with the changing times.

5.1. The Birth of Insurance

The concept of insurance is as old as human civilization itself. Originating from the need to mitigate risks, it can be traced back to ancient Chinese and Babylonian civilizations. In China, merchants distributing their wares across multiple vessels to spread the risk authenticated the earliest practice of insurance. Simultaneously, in Babylon, traders used the Hammurabi Code—an ancient law that worked somewhat like modern day insurance—to limit losses.

The concept gained more structure during the age of great maritime explorations. The widespread usage of sea loans and bottomry contracts (a practice where the vessel and its cargo served as collateral for loans) effectively protected merchants and ship owners. The advent of the modern insurance industry, however, can be traced back to the 17th-century coffee houses of London where the idea of pooling resources to compensate for losses gained popularity, paving the way for the establishment of pioneering insurance companies such as Lloyd's of London.

5.2. The Advent of Automobile and Health Insurance

With the turn of the 20th century, insurance expanded into new territories. Two pivotal developments were the advent of automobile and health insurance. With automobiles increasingly becoming a commonplace, accident risks escalated. This led to the introduction of the first comprehensive auto insurance policy in 1898. Simultaneously, social changes and technological advancements in medicine necessitated the need for health insurance. Hospitals and medical service corporations introduced prepaid health plans—a precursor to the modern-day health insurance.

5.3. Regulatory Changes

The industry underwent significant changes with regulatory developments during the mid-20th century. Countries started establishing regulatory bodies, ensuring solvency standards, and enforcing fair practices. The McCarran-Ferguson Act in the U.S., for example, gave states the right to regulate insurance while ensuring federal antitrust laws apply to the industry only to a limited extent.

5.4. Technological Disruption

The closing decades of the 20th century and the dawn of the 21st century marked the era of technological revolution in insurance. As technology started redefining all aspects of life, the industry adapted by deploying technologies like data analytics and later artificial intelligence and machine learninge. This enabled underwriting precision, cost reduction, improved customer service, and fraud detection.

5.5. Digitization and Insurtech

The advent of the internet supercharged the insurance industry's digitization. Insurtech, where technology is used to maximize the efficiency of insurance models, emerged. Start-ups and established firms alike began leveraging technologies like big data, IoT, predictive analytics, RPA (Robotic Process Automation), telematics, and much more. Direct-to-consumer (DTC) products gained momentum, transforming conventional broker-based models.

5.6. The Blockchain Era

Amid the continuing evolution, firmly stepping into the scene is the phenomenon of blockchain, set to redefine the industry once again. The resilience, security, transparency, and efficiency provided by this novel technology align perfectly with the core principles of insurance, offering endless possibilities for innovation and better service delivery.

The convergence of blockchain with other technologies like IoT and AI could potentially morph the industry to unprecedented heights. From smart contracts that simplify and expedite claims processing to disintermediation resulting in cost-efficiency and enhanced customer experience, blockchain is heralding a new age in insurance.

In conclusion, the evolution of the insurance industry reflects a fascinating journey laced with adaptation, innovation, and transformation. Yet, the journey is far from over. With the dawn of decentralized blockchain platforms, another significant turn in the evolution of insurance is well underway, promising a resilient, agile, and customer-centric model set to revolutionize insurance like never before. The exploration of this merger and the potentials it holds form the crux of the subsequent chapters.

Chapter 6. Blockchain Meets Insurance: A Momentous Intersection

The advent of blockchain technology has been hailed as a game-changer for numerous sectors, none more so than the insurance industry. Blockchain's promise of decentralization, transparency, and immutability could make it a fundamental tool for improving ease of doing business, enhancing security, and reducing fraudulent activities in the insurance sector.

6.1. The Early Alignment

Like the dawn of any substantial union, the early alignment of blockchain and insurance was first defined by curiosity and exploration rather than implementation. It is essential to understand that the insurance industry, a sector built on the exchange and protection of value, saw an appealing prospect in blockchain—a technology premised on the secure and immutable exchange of value. The natural congruence of these entities piqued interest from around the globe, driving exploratory studies, products, and platforms to delve into the fundamentals of blockchain, its potential use cases, and the challenges it faced in mainstream adoption.

6.2. Understanding Blockchain

To comprehend why blockchain is seen as such an impactful tool in the insurance industry, we first need to delve into the inner mechanisms powering this technology. At its essence, a blockchain is a digital ledger that is decentralized, secure, and transparent. Illustrious for its fundamental role in powering cryptocurrencies like Bitcoin, blockchain's capabilities stretch far beyond the digital currency realm.

A blockchain is a chain of blocks (hence the term), where each block carries information about transactions. All the parties involved in the network can view the information written on the blockchain. Once written on a block, the information cannot be altered or deleted, ensuring data integrity. Crucially, the system operates without the need for a central authority. Consequently, it eliminates the risk of a single point of failure and promises a robust, democratic, and trustworthy platform.

6.3. Blockchain - The Value Proposition for Insurance

Blockchain technology can aid the insurance industry in multiple ways. From streamlining processes to enhancing trust among parties, let's explore the blockchain's value proposition for insurance.

6.3.1. Transparency and Trust

Blockchain's transparency allows each participant in the chain to verify the records independently. This inherent transparency of blockchain has the potential to foster an unprecedented level of trust between insurers and their customers.

6.3.2. Fraud Detection and Risk Prevention

Blockchain's immutability helps in maintaining a tamper-evident log of all the transactions, thereby reducing the risk of fraud. For insurance companies, this can be a key feature in claim management to verify the authenticity of the claim and the claimant.

6.3.3. Efficiency and Cost Reduction

Blockchain encourages automation through smart contracts—self-executing contracts with the rules of the agreement directly written into the code. This not only expedites claim settlements but also significantly reduces administrative costs.

6.4. Case Studies: Where Blockchain Meets Insurance

The theoretical applications of blockchain in insurance are grand, but how does it play out in the real world? Let's take a look at some industry case studies.

6.4.1. B3i's Blockchain Initiative

The Blockchain Insurance Industry Initiative (B3i) was established by fifteen insurers and reinsurers, including Allianz, AIG, and Swiss Re, to explore the potential of blockchain. They developed a blockchain prototype for Property Cat XoL contracts, which helped streamline communication and transactions between insurers and reinsurers.

6.4.2. Etherisc's Flight Delay Insurance

Etherisc developed a decentralized application to automate flight delay insurance using blockchain. By leveraging smart contracts, the application provides instantaneous payouts to policyholders when their flights are delayed.

6.5. Conclusion: A Futuristic Policy

The convergence of blockchain technology and the insurance industry is carving out a new future for insurers and consumers alike. While the industry is still in its infancy in terms of blockchain adoption, the promise is real, and the enthusiasm is palpable. It's the dawn of a new era where trust, transparency, and security are the new norms, all courtesy of blockchain, the revolutionary technology underpinning this seismic shift.

Chapter 7. Key Use Cases: Blockchain in the Insurance Sector

The adoption of blockchain technology in the insurance sector has led to a significant shift in how insurance operations are conducted. Several use cases have emerged that underscore the potential the technology holds in the advancement of this sector.

7.1. Claim Processing and Fraud Detection

One of the primary uses of blockchain technology in insurance revolves around claim processing and fraud detection. Blockchain, with its unique attribute of data immutability, ensures transactions cannot be altered or deleted, creating a secure environment to store and verify information.

Traditional insurance claim processes are often riddled with lengthy procedures and a lack of transparency, leading to slow claim resolutions, and an increased likelihood of fraud. Blockchain's distributed ledger technology can introduce a greater level of transparency, speed, and efficiency to this process.

An insurance blockchain can record claims in a transparent and secure way, reducing the chances of duplicate or false claims. Firms can use smart contracts to automate claim verification and payment processes based on agreed-upon conditions. These contracts would trigger themselves when validated by the required number of parties, thus eliminating the need for manual intervention, reducing processing time and error likelihood.

Blockchain can allow insurers to work collaboratively with third parties such as hospitals, auto-repair shops, and police departments to share the evidence almost instantaneously. This way, blockchain can help reduce time and costs while enhancing customer satisfaction.

7.2. Peer-to-Peer (P2P) Insurance

The concept of P2P insurance is not new, and its principles of mutualization and trust have always underpinned insurance. However, blockchain technology brings this concept into the digital age with decentralized platforms.

In a blockchain-based P2P insurance model, a group of individuals that share a risk form a mutual insurance pool. Smart contracts are used to automate the process of accepting premiums and disbursing claim payouts. This system eliminates the need for an insurance company or any other intermediary to manage the pool and claims.

Blockchain, by ensuring trust through transparency and traceability, enables the creation of P2P insurance networks where individuals can manage risk collectively. This approach can reduce costs and increase efficiency by eliminating overhead costs that are part of traditional insurance models.

7.3. Parametric Insurance and Smart Contracts

Parametric insurance, a type of insurance that automatically pays out when a pre-defined event occurs, is another key use case for blockchain. The policyholder and the insurer agree upon specific trigger conditions at the policy inception, such as a natural disaster occurring.

With blockchain technology, parametric insurance can become more autonomous and trustworthy. The agreed-upon conditions to be met are programmed into a smart contract, and data from reliable third-parties, providing evidence that the event indeed took place, can trigger the smart contract.

This autonomous and transparent process thus removes any doubts or discrepancies about the claim, ensuring swift and equitable compensation distribution. Blockchain, along with smart contracts, can ensure timely payout mechanisms that strengthen the insurer-insured relationship.

7.4. Microinsurance

Microinsurance, a system of low-value insurance policies designed for low-income individuals and communities, is another field that could immensely benefit from blockchain technology.

Under normal circumstances, it is not cost-effective for traditional insurance companies to offer these policies due to high administration and distribution costs. However, blockchain can step in to solve this issue. The transparency, speed, and low cost of blockchain transactions, along with automatic claim verification via smart contracts, could make micro-insurance more manageable and profitable to insurers and more accessible to those who need it most.

7.5. Reinsurance

Reinsurance, the practice where insurance companies share risks to protect themselves from significant losses, can also benefit from blockchain technology. Managing reinsurance contracts is an intricate process involving parties in numerous locations and jurisdictions, all of which need to verify vast quantities of data.

Through a shared, immutable ledger, blockchain can improve trust and transparency between insurers and reinsurers, facilitating secure and efficient information transfer. Smart contracts can also help automate substantial parts of the reinsurance process, leading to significant time and cost savings.

These use cases demonstrate that blockchain technology is primed to enrich and redefine the insurance sector. By enhancing security, operational efficiency, transparency, and customer satisfaction, it can provide solutions to traditional industry bottlenecks. As this technology continues to evolve, it is poised to unlock even more opportunities in the insurance landscape.

Chapter 8. Challenges and Opportunities: Blockchain Adoption in Insurance

In the pursuit of understanding blockchain adoption in the insurance industry, one must symmetrically examine both its challenges and the opportunities it brings along. This dual-lens evaluation ensures a comprehensive preparedness for incorporating blockchain into the industry.

8.1. The Allure of Blockchain for Insurance

Sophisticated and secure, blockchain is the technological darling of the present era, renowned for its notable capabilities such as transactional transparency and the elimination of intermediaries. The insurance sector, intrinsically complex with its multiplicity of intermediaries, heavy dependence on legacy systems, and numerous manual processes, can gain tremendously from the revolutionary power of blockchain.

The key attractions of blockchain lie in decentralization, immutability of records, smart contracts, enhanced security, streamlined administrative procedures, and lower costs. These features have the potential to push the insurance industry into a new era of efficiency, trust, and customer satisfaction.

8.2. Focusing the Lens on Insurtech

In order to appreciate the full magnitude of the transformation, allow us to delve deeper into blockchain's implications for insurtech.

The paramount promise of blockchain in insurtech lies within smart contracts. These are self-executing contracts with terms of the agreement embedded in the code. They automatically execute actions such as payment processing when certain conditions are met, reducing friction in the process and making claim settlements faster and more transparent.

Blockchain serves to enrich the customer experience by underpinning transparency and reducing settlement times, with the blockchain's immutability demonstrating the absence of fraudulent activity. Furthermore, blockchain-enabled peer-to-peer (P2P) insurance or syndicates could give rise to collective risk-pooling models, further revolutionizing the industry and lending it a participatory flavor.

In the segment of health insurance, blockchain's secure, interoperable data sharing mechanism can be transformative. It allows healthcare providers, insurers, and patients to create, access, and update medical records on secure platforms, enhancing overall health service delivery.

8.3. Blockchain: The Challenges Ahead

While the above capabilities hint at a future full of promise, embedding blockchain into the insurance industry's complex fabric comes with a set of challenges.

Firstly, achieving comprehensive knowledge and understanding of blockchain's potential and its implications is a hurdle. Existing skills gaps and the absence of qualified personnel make it hard to implement and manage blockchain technology.

Secondly, migration from legacy systems to blockchain-based platforms requires massive investments in terms of finance, time, and workforce. It also involves a risk - the potential returns from these investments are uncertain as of now since the technology remains nascent and is in the process of achieving its full potential.

Moreover, regulatory and legal aspects cast a shadow. Blockchain's intrinsic characteristics of decentralization and anonymity complicate regulatory oversight. It also prompts questions around the legal validity of smart contracts, consumer protection, data privacy, and potential misuse.

8.4. Navigating Regulatory Ambiguities

Regulatory scrutiny on blockchain's implementation in the insurance industry is necessary, primarily to ensure compliance with data protection regulations. The immutable nature of blockchain, while being one of its principal strengths, also introduces the problem of 'right to be forgotten'. It's a requirement under GDPR for deleting personal data, indicating the need for careful design and management of blockchain networks.

Moreover, smart contracts, one of the revolutionary features of blockchain implementation, lack a legal framework. Clarifying the legal position of these digital agreements is paramount to ensure their appropriate use.

Achieving such regulatory clarity requires proactive engagement between blockchain innovators, insurers, and regulators to identify potential issues and develop practical solutions.

8.5. Metamorphosis: An Industry on the Precipice

In the grand scheme, blockchain can elevate efficiency, transparency, and accuracy within the insurance industry. Pushing through the challenges to seize upon these opportunities entails an enormous task, yet holds the promise of significant rewards.

Blockchain's adoption necessitates a symbiosis of blockchain technologists, insurance sector professionals, regulators, and other stakeholders. Working together, they can develop standards, regulatory guidelines, and best practice frameworks for successful blockchain integration.

As the wheel turns on blockchain adoption within insurance, it is essential to maintain a balanced view, understanding the challenges as much as the opportunities, to ensure that this promising technology is leveraged to its fullest potential and not allowed to become a missed opportunity. Furthermore, blockchain is not the panacea for all problems within insurance, nor is it appropriate for every process. Identifying its best applications within the industry is as crucial as mitigating its potential issues.

This chapter, therefore, calls for a keen understanding and accurate interpretation of the promised opportunities and outlined challenges. Marked with these insights, insurance, as we grasp it today, is set to embark on a revolutionary voyage, altering the conventional and sailing towards a promising, blockchain-infused horizon.

In conclusion, blockchain bears the torch that could kindle the dawn of a new age of technological innovation in insurance, where opportunities for improvement, efficiency, and vast potential for growth are recognized and seized upon while skilfully navigating the challenges and potential risks. This balance will set the sail for the journey towards successful blockchain adoption in the insurance industry.

Chapter 9. Leading Innovators: Blockchain-driven Insurance Platforms

As the technologic tides turn, we meet at the crest of a new wave: decentralized blockchain platforms reimagining the "business as usual" model of insurance. Leading innovators across the globe are developing and implementing these systems with impressive results. Their effects will reverberate throughout the insurance industry in unprecedented ways, necessitating a deeper comprehension of those platforms shaping the future.

9.1. Pioneering Enterprises On the Forefront

A host of new companies have emerged, distinguishing themselves as front-runners in investing, iterating, and implementing blockchain technology in their operations. These include the likes of Etherisc, Fizzy AXA, and Black Insurance, among others.

Etherisc has designed a pioneering model for decentralized insurance applications. This platform utilizes smart contracts to govern and execute insurance policies, eliminating intermediaries for a customer-centric autonomy over claims. Customers purchase an insurance policy governed by a smart contract. When a claim-triggering event occurs, the contract automatically executes the claim disbursement, reducing the typical delay and subjectivity involved in the traditional claims process.

Fizzy AXA offers another exciting foray into the blockchain world. This ambitious project from French global insurance giant, AXA, aims to simplify flight delay insurance. By combining blockchain technology and automated smart contracts, Fizzy AXA, upon a delay of more than two hours, triggers compensation to the policyholder without any claims filing.

Black Insurance ventures into the realm of investment and underwriting using blockchain. Underwriters and brokers can operate on the platform while investors provide capital for insurance risks. This model effectively bridges the gap between investors and brokers by streamlining the cumbersome process of policy origination, negotiation, and execution.

9.2. Underlying Technologies at Play

Understanding these innovative platforms presupposes comprehension of the underlying technologies driving them. Key components include blockchain, smart contracts, and distributed ledger technology.

Blockchain acts as a decentralized database, powered by myriad nodes that verify and record transactions into 'blocks.' These blocks interconnect into a chain, ensuring tamper-proof and transparent transactions. This inherent transparency and security has found its utility in sectors ever-dependent on trust, such as insurance.

Smart contracts, a subset of blockchain technology, automate contractual agreements. By encoding terms and conditions into a smart contract, this self-executing piece of software automatically performs prescribed actions when certain conditions are met. As a result, smart contracts eliminate middlemen, reduce cost, and promote efficiency with their use of blockchain's transparent and immutable nature.

The broad umbrella under which both blockchain and smart contracts fall is distributed ledger technology (DLT). DLT offers multiple parties simultaneous access to a continuously updated digital system that records all transactions. Within this ledger, each new transaction verifies and solidifies the ones before it, creating an indelible and transparent history that virtually eliminates the risk of fraud.

9.3. Opportunities and Challenges

Blockchain technology in insurance heralds a seismic shift in opportunity but must grapple with challenges along the path to widespread adoption.

Eliminating intermediaries and reducing frictions has significant implications for operational efficiency and cost reduction. Blockchain-based ecosystems like Etherisc, Fizzy AXA, and Black Insurance attest to the possibility of instantaneous policy issuance, claim validation, and payment disbursement.

On the other hand, a behemoth challenge that the industry grapples with is explaining complex and abstract blockchain technology to consumers and professionals alike. Insurers have to find a way to translate tech jargon into a language all stakeholders understand.

Further, blockchain technology's relative infancy presents a regulatory challenge. Existing legal structures and regulatory guidelines fail to fully capture blockchain's unique aspects. Until a clear regulatory framework emerges, the promise of decentralization remains clouded in ambiguity.

9.4. Toward the Future

Leading innovators leveraging decentralized blockchain platforms are trailblazing the insurance industry's path forward. Pioneers like Etherisc, Fizzy AXA, and Black Insurance exploit blockchain's capabilities with their innovative business models. Underneath the operations lie the intricate technologies of blockchain, smart contracts, and distributed ledger technology, fueling the secure and streamlined future of insurance.

Significant challenges, however, continue to exist. Wide-scale education and regulatory adjustments are requisite for blockchain technology's insurance adoption. Despite these obstacles, the industry barrels forth, seeding a new era of digital transformation underwritten by blockchain technology. The insurance industry as we know it waits in anticipation as it adjusts its sails to the winds of profound innovation.

In conclusion, the age of blockchain-driven insurance platforms has dawned. The course charted by pioneering players, while far from smooth sailing, promises a future marked by increased transparency, efficiency, and democratization. Whether you're an industry professional, policyholder, or investor, tune in; the blockchain revolution has only just begun.

Chapter 10. Regulation Landscape: Governing Blockchains in Insurance

To confront the intricate entanglement of technology, law, and insurance that comes with the regulation of blockchain in insurance, we first need a comprehensive understanding of what we are dealing with. The combination of digital data records with cryptographic security – that's the concept of blockchain, a decentralized public ledger of transactions that is transparent, secure, and immutable.

Blockchain technology has catalyzed a seismic shift in a multitude of industries, with the insurance sector among those leading the charge. This shift promises immense potential, but it also presents a profound challenge to existing regulatory mechanisms—hence the rising importance of blockchain regulation within the insurance industry.

10.1. The Decentralized Nature of Blockchain

At the heart of the blockchain framework lies the decentralization of control. This lack of a central authority acts as both a boon and a bane. While it fuels transparency and reduces the risk of fraud, it raises colossal regulatory challenges. A dilemma arises - how can a decentralized system be brought under any central authority's control or conform to regulation?

Moreover, the global reach and ubiquity of blockchain technology further complicate regulatory efforts. How are regulators to address a technology that operates borderlessly when even the basic legal definition of a 'blockchain transaction' differs from country to country?

10.2. Regulatory Approach: Adaptation and Implementation

Regulators have responded by adopting two distinct methods: adapting current regulations to include blockchain or implementing new regulations specifically designed for blockchain.

The adaptation strategy assesses how existing laws or regulations apply to blockchain transactions. This mechanism staves off the need for additional, possibly cumbersome, legislation. However, it may forcibly subject the technology to frameworks that do not entirely suit its nature.

In contrast, the implementation of blockchain-specific regulations provides a framework tailored to the unique aspects of blockchain technology. Nevertheless, this approach brings its own challenges as regulators grapple with the fast-paced development of the technology and struggle to legislate proactively.

10.3. Jurisdictional Challenges and Global Regulatory Response

As blockchain operates on a global scale, the legal jurisdiction becomes a sticky point. Some countries have adopted a welcoming approach to blockchain, while others present a much more stringent regulatory environment.

For instance, Malta has sought to become a blockchain haven, introducing three new laws aimed at fostering a positive blockchain environment. Similarly, Switzerland has embraced blockchain technology, with Canton Zug becoming known as the 'Crypto Valley.'

Contrasting this, China has imposed remarkably stringent regulations, effectively banning any financial institutions from dealing with blockchain transactions.

These differing stances underline a crucial challenge – the lack of a uniform regulatory landscape. The implications of this discord for insurance companies employing blockchain are significant.

10.4. Specific Considerations for Insurance

When it comes to regulating blockchain within the insurance sector, several specific considerations come into play.

Insurers need to ensure that blockchain processes adhere to data protection and privacy regulations. GDPR, for instance, presents a significant challenge as it necessitates the right for data to be deleted - something not inherently possible within an immutable blockchain.

Secondly, the smart contracts that underpin many blockchain insurance applications need robust regulation to address issues such as contract law, clarity over obligations, and dispute resolution.

Thirdly, the international nature of blockchain raises challenges for enforcing regulation and where liability might lie in the event of disputes.

The blockchain revolution in insurance is underway, offering massive potential to revamp outdated systems and processes. However, a mindful approach is needed to surmount the regulatory challenges. This involves working with regulators to help them understand the opportunities and intricacies of blockchain technology and developing a legal framework that protects consumers without stifling innovation. As the regulatory landscape continues to evolve, so too will the role of blockchain in the insurance industry.

Chapter 11. Looking Ahead: The Future of Insurance with Blockchain

The future of insurance stands at the precipice of massive change, primarily driven by the explosive impact of blockchain technology. As industries across all sectors grapple with the challenge of digital transformation, insurance is expected to gain significantly from blockchain, the technology behind cryptocurrencies.

11.1. Blockchain: The Disruptor in Insurance

We can no longer deny the presence of blockchain in our world today. Bitcoin's inception in 2009 marked the birth of blockchain technology, and since then, it has found applications across multiple industries, from financial services to healthcare. Its adamantium-grade security attributes, combined with its intrinsic structure supporting transparency and immutability, has positioned it as an industry disruptor.

How might, then, blockchain disrupt and reshape the insurance landscape? Blockchain's decentralization aspect has the potential to simplify numerous processes in insurance. Insurance, by its very nature, involves an intricate web of stakeholders – insurers, insured parties, brokers, and third-party administrators. Each stakeholder maintains separate data silos, culminating in inefficiencies, redundancies, and increased costs. Blockchain's decentralized ledger can harmonize these records, substantially reducing duplication and errors.

On the aspect of trust, blockchain has the potential to instill greater confidence among stakeholders. If insurance is considered as a business of trust, the transparency and immutability offered by blockchain can make trust inherent in every transaction. Much of the friction in insurance arises from the scepticism over fraudulent claims, which, when detected, often entail tedious investigations. However, a blockchain-based system could eliminate or drastically reduce these instances, expediting claim settlements.

11.2. Impact of Blockchain on Key Insurance Areas

Let's explore some insurance sectors set for disruption due to blockchain technology.

11.2.1. Claims Processing

Claims processing often involves complex procedures and takes considerable time due to the verification of documents, the need for third-party services, and the manual entry of data. Blockchain can automate much of this process using smart contracts - self-executing contracts with the terms of agreement written into code, minimizing errors and making the process less time-consuming.

11.2.2. Underwriting

Underwriting involves assessing risks and deciding the premiums to be charged. Blockchain can significantly automate this process by collating customer-related data from various sources and using machine learning algorithms. This reduces human error and bias, offering a more accurate risk analysis.

11.2.3. Fraud Detection

Insurance fraud causes significant loss to insurance companies every year. Blockchain's ability to provide a transparent and immutable ledger of transactions can facilitate the detection and prevention of fraudulent activities, thereby saving significant costs.

11.2.4. Reinsurance

In reinsurance, blockchain can streamline data transfer between insurers and reinsurers through a shared ledger. This will effectively simplify the process, reducing associated administrative costs and improving efficiency.

11.3. Potential Challenges

As promising as blockchain sounds, several challenges can't be overlooked. The novelty of the technology itself presents questions about its long-term viability. Also, implementation of blockchain-based solutions involves a complete overhaul of legacy systems, which carries financial implications and a learning curve for employees. Data privacy is another concern, particularly considering the global legal landscape with regulations like GDPR. Additionally, widespread adoption of blockchain in insurance will require regulation, standardization, and interoperability across different blockchain systems. Understanding, addressing, and resolving these challenges will be crucial in realizing the full potential of blockchain technology for the insurance industry.

11.4. Conclusion

The advent of blockchain technology has presented the insurance industry with the potential for unprecedented growth and efficiencies. However, as with any new technology, there are challenges ahead that need to be addressed and navigated. The question is not 'if' but 'when' the industry will fully embrace blockchain, and those companies that are proactive in doing so will have a competitive advantage, setting the industry standards of tomorrow and defining what customer experience in insurance looks like in the future. While the journey may seem complicated, the potential rewards are too large to ignore. The future seems set to be written on the blockchain.

www.ingramcontent.com/pod-product-compliance
Lightning Source LLC
Chambersburg PA
CBHW062309290526
45794CB00006B/2736